The Lily Pad and the Dragonfly

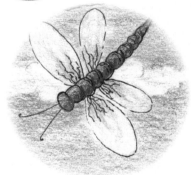

A Story of Spiritual Enlightenment as told by Arden L. Johnson

Interpreted by Heidi A. Mengis

AuthorHouse™
1663 Liberty Drive
Bloomington, IN 47403
www.authorhouse.com
Phone: 833-262-8899

Because of the dynamic nature of the Internet, any web addresses or links contained in this book may have changed
since publication and may no longer be valid. The views expressed in this work are solely those of the author and do not
necessarily reflect the views of the publisher, and the publisher hereby disclaims any responsibility for them.

This book is printed on acid-free paper.

ISBN: 978-1-4490-2535-9 (sc)
ISBN: 978-1-4685-8959-7 (e)

Print information available on the last page.

Published by AuthorHouse   12/10/2024

authorHOUSE®

There was a colony of water bugs living in a muddy pond. They enjoyed playing together, swimming around, all the things that water bugs like to do.

As the summer went on, they realized that their numbers were diminishing and there were fewer and fewer of them. So, those who remained got together and decided what ever this strange mystery was that was causing some of them to disappear, if it ever happened to them- to any of them- they would come back and let the others know what the mystery was all about.

A few days later, one of the water bugs had this strange urge to swim away. He swam away and found a lily pad and he climbed up the stalk of the lily pad. When he reached the surface, above the water; he spread himself out on the soft lily pad to lie in the sun. He lay there in the sun for quite some time. While he was lying there, he fell asleep. Hours, perhaps even days later his body began to shake.

It was a convulsion of sort and his body burst open and out of that came a new creature. The creature had large wings and huge eyes, entirely different from that of the water bug. When exposed to the sun he soon dried, and out of the shell came a dragonfly.

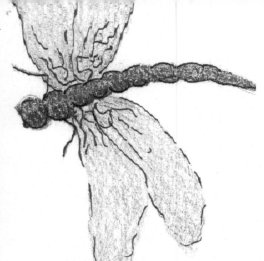

The dragonfly stayed on the lily pad for just a moment and then realized that with these HUGE wings he could fly. So, he took off and with his large eyes he could see things he had never seen before. He flew and flew; he went all over the place. It seemed like there weren't any limits as to where he could go or what he could see. He flew all day and discovered new things he never knew existed.

At the close of the day, he was exhausted from all of his new adventures and he came to rest on a beautiful rose. What a wonderful place to fold up his wings, fall asleep and spend the night. He closed his wings and remembered the promise he had made to his water bug friends.

He decided to fly back to the lily pad. When he arrived, there was his old shell, all dried up. He knew that the only way he could go back and tell his friends would be to go back into that old body and turn back into a water bug. He decided no way; this new life that he had was so much greater, so much better in every way that there was no way he was going back to be a water bug again.

So, he walked over to the edge of the lily pad and looked down to see his friends swimming around, playing and having fun. He got a tear in his eye and he wished that somehow he could go back and tell them what a wonderful thing had happened. He simply looked at them and said "you'll have to wait your turn and then you will understand."

I think that's the way it is. What happens to us beyond this life is so different from the life we know, that there's no way to describe it. It's so much better, so much more beautiful in every way.

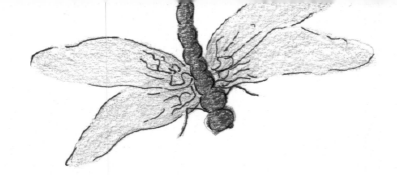

The Bible tells us God takes care of all things: all creatures, birds, animals and, I think, water bugs and dragonflies. If God can turn a water bug into a dragonfly, if God is willing to change a fuzzy caterpillar into a beautiful butterfly: won't He take care of us.

When our time comes to close out this life, we all have something a lot better to look forward to. God will take care of us and God will give us a life that is just so fantastic, it's beyond words to describe.

Printed in the United States
by Baker & Taylor Publisher Services